total surrender

walking by faith

Gene Schuyler

Total Surrender

First Printing, September 2011

ISBN: 978-0-6155115-4-2

Scripture quotations are from the King James Version of the Bible unless otherwise stated.

Printed in the United States of America

Cover photo: Iakov Kalinin / shutterstock.com

❧ *Dedication* ❧

———

I have to dedicate this work to my wonderful wife, Marie. She has been my faithful wife through these fifty-two years of marriage and has given me four precious children. When we lost our little girl, Rebecca, her faith was so strong at a time when other mothers would retreat and even stop serving the Lord. Marie's love for the Lord has never wavered no matter where we went in the ministry. She never challenged me when I moved her from place to place and uprooted her home and the children. So many times when I was ready to give up she was the one who challenged me. She always told me that "God makes no mistakes and I should never quit." She has been and still is my best friend; a teacher of the Word to her peers, dedicated to her church and the ministry that she began at our present church, ("Tennis Shoes for Christ"), and the most dedicated prayer warrior that I have even known.

I also want to thank my children for putting up with me through the early years of my ministry and all the moves that they made with me and having no real "home place" and "old" friends from their youth and following me as I followed my Lord's leadership.

Thank you Donny, now a father and grandfather -

Thank you Donna, now a mother and grandmother -

Thank you Tracy, now a mother (no grandkids yet) -

Thank you for your love and patience and understanding, even now, as I continue my walk by Faith.

❧

~ *In Loving Memory* ~

Rebecca Iona Schuyler

Born: August 28, 1975

Went to be with the Lord: April 15, 1977

Rebecca was our miracle baby born when we thought our days of having children were over. What a beautiful smile, loving disposition and a heart that won over every one that ever held her.

Her time was short here on earth, but in only twenty months she captured the hearts of my personal family and the family of Bible Baptist Temple.

The day will come for us to be together again. As David of old said, "can I bring him back again? I shall go to him, but he shall not return to me" (II Samuel 11:23 NASB).

One day Marie and I along with Donny, Donna and Tracy will be reunited with our Rebecca and we will never be separated again.

~

❧ *Table of Contents* ❧

❧ *Foreword* ❧

by Evangelist Junior Hill

W. S. Borden wisely said, "Prayer is weakness leaning on omnipotence."

For men and women of faith, prayer is the desperate cry of the helpless lifted up to the attentive ear of the Helper. Anything that affords a better understanding of that wonderful process of intercession is always welcome news. That's why this delightful book by Gene Schuyler is such a benediction of grace.

He not only has given us some helpful insights into the meaning of prayer, but better yet, he shares with the reader encouraging examples and illustrations of answered prayers taken from his own ministry of more than forty years. I found perusing these pages to be an unusually pleasurable experience. Reading what the Lord has done in the life of Gene and his dear wife, Marie, has encouraged me to believe that my Heavenly Father will do the same for me.

These are not words of a novice who has viewed prayer from the comfort of the sidelines, but rather the reassuring reports of one who has been through the rigorous conflicts of almost a half century of ministry. With refreshing humbleness, he has drawn back the drapes and given us a brief glimpse of his personal journey with the Lord. It is a heartening behind the scenes view of what God has done for Gene Schuyler - and not what Gene Schuyler has done for God.

I am glad we have this book, and I sincerely pray that it will find its way into the hands of many, many others who will be as blessed by its reading as this writer has been.

❧

❧ *Preface* ❧

FULL SURRENDER: Walking by FAITH and PRAYER

Prayers answered in the Schuyler family in their walk with Jesus for their forty plus years of ministry.

"And it came to pass, as He was praying in a certain place, that when He ceased, one of His disciples said to Him, Lord, teach us to pray" (Luke 11:1).

After being saved for over 55 years I still feel the need of being taught to pray. Andrew Murray said, "At first there is no work appears so simple; later on, none that is more difficult; and the confession is forced from us: We know not how to pray as we ought. It is true we have God's Word, with its clear and sure promises; but, sin has so darkened our mind, that we know not always how to apply the Word. In spiritual things we do not always seek the most needful things, or fail in praying according to the law of the sanctuary. In temporal things we are still less able to avail ourselves of the wonderful liberty our Father has given us to ask what we need. And even when we know what to ask, how much there is still needed to make prayer acceptable. It must be to the glory of God, in full surrender to His will, in full assurance of faith, in the name of Jesus, and with a perseverance that, if need be, refuses to be denied. All this must be learned. It can only be learned in the school of much prayer, for practice makes perfect. Amid the painful consciousness of ignorance and unworthiness, in the struggle between believing and doubting, the heavenly art of effectual prayer is learned. Because, even when we do not remember it, there is One, the Beginner and Finisher of faith and prayer, who watches over our praying, and sees to it that in all who trust Him for it their education in the school of prayer shall be carried on to perfection. Let but the deep undertone of all our prayer be the teachable - that comes from a sense of ignorance, and from faith in Him as a perfect teacher, and we may be sure we shall be taught, we shall learn to pray in power. Yes, we may depend upon it, HE teaches to pray."

"Ask, and it shall be given you; seek, and ye shall find; knock and it shall be opened unto you: for every one that asketh receiveth and he that seeketh findeth; and to him that knocketh it shall opened" (Matthew 7:7-8). "Ye ask, and receive not, because ye ask amiss" (James 4:3).

In the three words that our Lord uses, *ask, seek, knock,* there are great differences in meaning. The first, ASK, refers to the gifts we pray for. But I may ask and receive the gift without the Giver. Through the word, SEEK, Christ assures me that I can find Him. But it is not enough to find God in time of need; one must come to an abiding fellowship. KNOCK speaks of admission to dwell with Him and in Him. It was Andrew Murray that said, "Asking and receiving the gift would thus lead to seeking and finding the Giver, and this again to the knocking and opening of the door of the Father's home and love. One thing is sure, the Lord does want us to count most certainly on it that asking, seeking, knocking, cannot be in vain: receiving an answer, finding God, the opened heart and home of God, are the certain fruit of prayer."

My life, before surrendering to full-time ministry, was one of mediocre prayer unless I really wanted something or was in a time of great need. It was not until I surrendered to enter the ministry in 1966 that my walk with God and my prayer life became a vital part of my personal life and my family.

This book is not about doctrine or how to prepare sermons. It is about how God answered prayer during over 43 years of serving our Savior. Being a full-time servant of our Lord Jesus Christ is the most wonderful life one could ever hope to experience.

Let me begin by giving a definition of prayer. "Prayer projects faith on God, and God on the world." Only God can move mountains, but faith and prayer move God. In His cursing of the fig tree our Lord demonstrated His power. Following that, He proceeded to declare that large powers were committed to faith and prayer, not in order to kill but to make alive, not to blast but to bless.

Also, faith is a vital part of prayer, i.e. "Faith does the impossible because it brings God to undertake for us and nothing is impossible with God. How great, without qualification or limitation, is the power of faith!"

As you read this book it may seem to you that I have been a failure in my ministry because of my many moves, but I know that God makes and made no mistakes. When I think of all those that we have met during these forty-three years of following my call from the Lord and the hundreds of souls that have come to know Christ as their Savior it has been worth all the hurts and heartaches. "To God be the glory!"

❧

❧ *Acknowledgements* ❧

I am so thankful to my former pastor, William Kingston, who is now in heaven. His dedication to keeping me on the right path after I got saved was a great blessing to me.

I am thankful for the men that taught me at Fruitland Baptist Bible Institute. Special thanks go to Dr. John Rymer who taught me how to study God's Word and to preach its truth in its entirety. Dr. Bobby Graham taught me how to be a faithful and fearless soul winner. Dr. John O'Cain allowed me to preach many times in his pulpit which gave me experience in presenting the gospel and also helped me in my pulpit manners. Special thanks go to Dr. Alex Booth, who now is in Heaven. Dr. Booth was the academic dean of Fruitland when I was a student. He always kept up with me as my ministry progressed giving me much encouragement and challenging me to go beyond my education at Fruitland to complete my doctorate in Christian Education. I am thankful to him for giving me so many opportunities to preach during my years at Fruitland and for recommending me to the first church that I was to pastor. I look forward to our reunion in heaven.

I also want thank Dr. Larry Upchurch, my present pastor and friend for over forty years, for his encouragement and for allowing me to serve with him and the wonderful members of Mid-Way Baptist Church of Raleigh, N.C., for these many years.

Thank you, Dr. Bill Bowyer, for being a listening arm for me many times and being a prayer partner.

A special thanks to Evangelist Junior Hill for being so kind to read this book before publication and for the guidance he gave me as well. I am also thankful for his faithfulness for all the years he has served His Savior and Lord.

&

❧ *Total Surrender* ❧

Walking by Faith

❧ *Introduction* ❧

E. M. Bounds said, "Obedience to God counts tremend-ously in the realm of prayer. This fact cannot be emphasized too much or too often. To plead for a religious faith which tolerates sinning is to cut the ground from under the feet of effectual praying. To excuse sinning by the plea that obedience to God is not possible to unregenerate men is to discount the character of the new birth, and to place men where effective praying is not possible. At one time Jesus broke out with a very pertinent and personal question, striking right to the core of disobedience, when he said: 'Why call ye me, Lord, Lord, and do not the things I say?' He, who would pray, must obey. He, who would get anything out of his prayers, must be in perfect harmony with God. Prayer puts into those who sincerely pray a spirit of obedience, for the spirit of disobedience is not of God and belongs not to God's praying hosts.

An obedient life is a great help to prayer. In fact, an obedient life is a necessity to prayer, to the sort which accomplishes things. The absence of an obedient life makes prayer an empty performance, a mere misnomer. A penitent sinner seeks pardon and salvation and has an answer to his prayers even with a life stained and debauched with sin. But God's royal intercessors come before him with royal lives. Holy living promotes holy praying. God's intercessors 'lift up holy hands,' the symbols of righteous, obedient lives."

❧

1

Marie's Prayer for My Life

CHAPTER ONE

⟜

I was born in Florence, South Carolina, on July 12, 1939, just before the beginning of World War II. I can remember the days of watching and listening to the roar of US Army Air Corps Bombers flying over my home so very close that you could see the star on the wing and the numbers brightly beaming. I remember many nights listening to my aunts talk about their husbands in the army overseas fighting and one of my aunts working at the Florence Air Field packing parachutes. I remember listening to the families in my neighborhood talking about when their loved ones would come home. Many a night the air raid sirens would sound and the "black shades" had to be pulled down so no lights would be seen from above and to hear the "Air raid wardens" sound their whistles and call "all lights out." This also was a time when the local physicians would make house calls, I know, for my doctor came to stay with me once for many hours due to my having the "croup."

One of the most memorable times during this time was when one of my neighbor's sons was coming home from the war, and hearing her running up and down the street, screaming to the top of her voice, "Odell, is coming home." I also remember my next door neighbor receiving word that her brother was killed in action and how our neighborhood came together. I can also remember the night my dad was drafted and how my mother broke down as he left for induction. He was only gone around four days when the war ended and he never had to serve. I remember my dad saying he wished he had been one to help fight for his country. But to me, my dad was a hero for he kept the home front safe with his dedication to his country.

I also remember, as a five year old, that church was a big part of my life as a child. We only lived a block away from our church and I went to Sunday school every Sunday. The church during this time was open twenty-four hours every day for people to come in and pray.

I remember so well, how one of our families had two sons in the US Army Air Corps and hearing that one was shot down and survived. It was at church that I heard about Jesus and His love for the world and where I got involved in reading and loving God's Word.

As a junior in Sunday school, I got involved in the "sword drills" and even won the area title in the contest, but I was never presented the need of the gospel for myself through the years of my childhood.

At the age of fourteen, my parents started attending another Baptist church; I guess it was because the pastor of our old church left and my parents were invited to attend a rather new church in the area, so we did. It was there as a young teenager that I heard more about having a personal relationship with Christ. It was on a Sunday night that I was saved at the age of sixteen, along with my cousin. The pastor introduced us to the church and told them about our decision. He also shared that he believed "One of these young men will become a preacher." Well, I certainly was not the "one" that would. How wrong I was, for within a few weeks God began to work on my heart and I felt His call and publicly announced it in church.

From that point on, I began to seek the Word of God with great intensity and just could not get enough of His Word. Time went on and I was involved in the "Youth for Christ" ministry along with my then girl friend, Marie, now my wife. I even started preaching. I still have the outline entitled, "The Worst Thing That Can Happen to a Teenager," and I remember that it only lasted about 10 minutes. I began leading the music in our church and on many occasions had the privilege of preaching at "Youth for Christ" meetings around the area. Later on, a great man came into my life as my pastor, William Kingston. He taught me how to really study God's Word and how prayer should be a vital part of the ministry.

It was during that time that I saw the importance of prayer and the part it would play in my life, my future ministry and all the decisions that I would have to make. Second Corinthians 5:7 says, "For we walk by faith, not by sight."

Time went by so quickly during my teen years and I met a wonderful, beautiful, black haired, blue-eyed, five foot-two inch girl who became my wife. Marie and I have been married for fifty-two years. We became very involved with our church during those teen years and then Satan began to work on my life. Without going into detail, I had one great dream before I was saved. I longed to become a professional baseball player. The dream seemed to becoming true until at age fifteen I injured my arm. All hopes for a baseball career ended. I began to rebel and gave up going into the ministry. This is where Marie really stepped in with her strong prayer life, even before we were married.

In September of 1958 we were married. Marie was a senior in high school and she struggled with my call into the ministry. I left for Bible school in Texas and only stayed for two months. Being lonely and discouraged and yes, angry with my Savior for not letting me be successful in my dream of a professional baseball player. I left school and returned home to try to make something of my life. I went from job to job, making about fifty cents per hour at a fruit stand. That was not much for a married man. I made another attempt at a baseball career but failed due to my inability to play at the level needed. Once again I began to go from job to job. In one year alone I held over nine different jobs.

We began a family when our son was born in September of 1959 and then our first daughter came along in January of 1961. I was far from serving the Lord. My bitterness became stronger. I did not want anyone to be my friend. I preferred to be a loner. I became involved in playing "sand lot" baseball to keep my dream alive instead of getting involved in church. Marie stayed faithful to her Lord and prayed so hard that I would return to the Savior that I knew in my teen years. During this time, I continued to wander from job to job. I even started my own business which failed miserably. I was still trying to seek peace and purpose in life. In 1963 God opened up a great opportunity for me in the secular world for what I believed would be my future for the rest of my life. What I did not realize, Marie was praying hard every day that I would give up and surrender to the ministry that God had called me to back in 1955.

I worked as a delivery man for the local Ford dealership delivering parts. After work I went to college until eleven o'clock each night for six months. One day I saw an article in the local newspaper about a plant from Illinois that was going to relocate in the local area. They planned to start taking applications to train and hire the trainees. I got excited, applied and was accepted.

The days were long and hard. After completing the training I was interviewed and hired. It seemed that I was finally going to make something of myself. I remembered all of my young adult life what a fourth grade teacher told me one day during class. She said, *"Gene, you will never amount to anything."* I never seemed to get over such a negative statement, and it sure seemed like she had been right. Let me pause here to encourage you to never give up on your dream, calling or walk with Christ.

Well, I could not wait to get started. I was finally going to become a good husband and provider for my family. My wife would soon be able to quit work and be a stay-at-home mom.

Time went on and I was becoming quite successful in my career. My company chose me, after being with them for about one year, to have a documentary film made of my training and life's journey. The film was shot at a number of locations. They began at my home with my family at the breakfast table re-enacting the time I first heard of the plant coming to our area.

It then moved to the technical center where my training was re-enacted. What an experience that was with all the film crew following me around. There were even rumors that a "famous movie star was on campus." Some students wondered if James Dean was there. Filming continued throughout the plant showing my quick move up the ladder in the company.

My family and I had a private showing of the documentary. The film was later shared with the industrial world to show how someone could be trained in a field that he had never worked in and still become successful. I was at the top of the world, yet far away from the Lord.

As time went on, I became more self centered and attributed my success to my own ability. I did not see the need for church in my life. When asked by my wife and our pastor to get back in church, I became very bitter toward the church and even toward Marie, who stayed faithful. Week after week my wife attended church with the children, alone. The night that prayer finally changed my life was during a revival that my wife was attending.

Marie wanted me to go so bad, and began to put a little pressure on me to attend the revival. I retaliated in a very hateful way and even threatened her life if she went to the meeting. I told her that if she tried to go to church, I would cut all the tires on all four of the cars we had to keep her from going and her response was that she would walk. Then in a fit of anger, I said to her, "I will cut your legs out from under you." To my surprise she responded, "Then I will crawl." It was her words then that ripped my heart out when she said, "I will never stop praying for you." In anger, I told her to go on to church and take the children, but never come back! I will never forget those words said in hatred. Well, she went on to church and I sat alone, or at least I thought I was alone. I had forgotten that the HOLY SPIRIT was there. That night the only thing on television was a special program with Billy Graham preaching. I tried every channel and you guessed it, Billy Graham was the only program on. Not long into the program a sharp thunder cloud came up and a bolt of lightning came down my hallway. It stopped at the couch that I was sitting on and did I ever pay attention. I knew God was speaking to me. I repented on my knees and surrendered to Him to do whatever He wanted me to do. When I looked up the mark of the lightning was gone.

I prayed that Marie would hurry home after the services because I couldn't wait to tell her what had happened. She came straight home and when I told her what had happened, she began to weep uncontrollably when she said, "we had special prayer for you during the service." Talk about answered prayer! I am a walking example today of someone who owes his life to a prayer warrior.

I surrendered to the ministry the next Sunday and began my journey to fulfilling that call. I began to witness everyday at work and my fellow workers began to see the change in my life and my attitude of happiness. The desire to study God's Word again became my focus now, not my job. I remember one night while studying Galatians 2, verse twenty jumped out like a bolt of lightning that I put together a message and was so excited about it that when I finished it, around midnight, I rushed to my pastors house and woke him up and shared it with him. What a graceful man he was to be patient and kind to me to read it and then he requested that I preach it the following Wednesday night. I knew then, that God's call for my life was to preach His Word.

The next step was resigning my job even though my closest friends said that I was making a mistake. I began to look for the Bible school that God wanted me to attend. It didn't take long for God to lead me to the Fruitland Baptist Bible Institute for my training. Our prayers were really beginning to be fulfilled. We put our house on the market and it sold within two weeks. The school had an opening that was not there when I applied. They even had a room on campus. I began to see how prayer and faith work together.

☙

❧ 2 ❧

The Year Leading Up to Starting Bible School

CHAPTER TWO

&

I n 1966 on the Monday after I surrendered to full-time service, with apprehension I went to my superior to tell him about my decision. I also gave him a one year notice of my leaving the company. Now, as a supervisor of men, I knew that no company would entertain the idea of an employee giving a year's notice. Well, he was a Godly man listening to me intently and with compassion. After our conversation, we went to the vice-president of the company to tell him my story. To my surprise, the company accepted my notice of one year. Why give a one year notice? I wanted to be debt free as I entered school. With two children and a wife to support, school costs and other unknown needs, I did not want to go into debt.

The first thing we did was put our house on the market. We also sold a couple of cars within that first year. My wife and I began to pray about the selling them and within two weeks the house was sold and the two extra cars were sold within three months. My advice for over forty-three years as a pastor to young men, called by God to full time service, is never leave for school with debt, especially if they are married. My advice is to take as much time as necessary to become debt free before leaving for school. Why? Satan will use debt to defeat you. If you can't pay your bills, you cannot concentrate on your studies. You must take care of your family, if you are married. The world frowns on Bible students who do not pay their bills. I know that, because during my time at school, it was hard to establish financial credibility because of the many students in the past had faltered with the credit. So, be a good steward and one with a testimony.

Let me continue here for just a moment to share what the year was like during my preparation to leave. In the year at the plant, I had the privilege to witness to over 50% of the employees, many with salvation needs, family needs and even Christians who needed a closer walk with God. Most of the time during my lunch breaks and after work I would spend hours with men in prayer. All of this was an answer to prayer. I had prayed for God to use me and prepare me to enter the ministry of helping people. God sure opened those doors during that year.

It was also during this year that Satan did his work. So many times he would attack me with thoughts like "staying at the plant was more important and that I could reach so many more men there." Believe me, it sure was tempting since every month of that year, I got a small increase in salary. Yet, I knew God's call to full time service was real. I had said "**NO**" once, but not this time. This time it was **FULL SURRENDER!**

The time came to leave and what a day that was. You see, I had been one of the first fifteen that was hired at the opening of the plant and for three years I had the privilege of training many men. I had even become great friends with many of them. During that year so many would come up and share that they were praying for me and hated to see me leave. I had to "promise" to come back to see them from time to time.

CHAPTER TWO

The day came to leave the company and start out for school. That was a sad day for me in a way. I would be leaving men that I had grown up with in the secular world of work. It was a time when two men, Russell Cross and Chuck Powers, helped me to become a man and taught me how to become a leader. I had the privilege to lead many to Christ and helped many others to walk closer with their Lord. When the time came for me to finally leave, I was so surprised that the entire plant came to my work location, the "gear lab." What a sight to behold as hundreds of men came to face me. My dear friend and superior, Russell Cross, who is now with the Lord, made a short speech. Afterwards he said, "We have purchased two offering plates for you, since a preacher will surely need them." What a roar of laughter went throughout the building. Next they took up an offering and it was enough to pay for my first semester's tuition and all my books. What a blessing and another answer to prayer. It was also great assurance that God never fails when we follow His perfect will by Faith.

It was a sad day, yet a day that Marie and I had waited for. It was the beginning of what has now been over forty-three years of serving our Lord. We have never regretted one day of these forty-three years of prayer and waiting on the Lord.

This book can never reveal how many prayers God has answered for us. Yes, God did answer all of our prayers, not all on our time or as we desired, but in His time and according to His purpose for our lives.

ॐ

❧ 3 ❧

Walking by Prayer and Faith During Our Bible School Years

CHAPTER THREE

❧

A s I started off to school, it was not as difficult to leave the secular world as it was to leave my wife and two children behind, only to have them with me.

Let me pause here for a moment to share a very serious but humorous time on the way to Bible school. I had a bad habit that I did not want to give up and that was smoking, yes, smoking. I had gotten to the point that I was addicted to smoking three to four packs of cigarettes every day along with five to six pipes of tobacco.

I knew that I would have to give up this habit, if God was going to use me. The night that I left for school, all five hours of the car trip, I "lit up" and off I went. It was sometime around eight o'clock p.m. on I-26 in South Carolina that I was pulled over by a state patrol officer. I wasn't speeding. When he got out, he asked me, "Sir, Do you know that there is a great amount of smoke coming out of your car?" I assured him that I knew it and it was because I was smoking so many cigarettes that it looked like the car was on fire. He asked, "Why?" Being very embarrassed, I told him my plight. He just laughed and said, "Be careful, and stop smoking." Wow, what a terrible testimony!

I finally arrived at campus late in the night, found my room and settled into a new life. I was scared to death of the unknown and how God would use me.

There were no student apartments available on campus and we could not afford off campus living quarters. So, I stayed in the dormitories until an apartment became available. This was quite an experience for me, not having my wife with me.

For the first semester I commuted to and from school each week, leaving on Mondays and returning on Friday nights. It certainly was trying and tiring to say the least. Many great experiences were gained by being a "student on campus." I met many great fellow-students and found out that we all had the same things in common. You need to remember, I had to learn how to study all over and this took some doing! During my semester on campus I had the privilege of spending time with godly men that were my professors and friends. There were men as Dr. James Walker, Dr. Alex Booth, who followed my ministry until his going home to be with the Lord many years later, and Dr. John Rymer, who challenged me to become a student of the Word in its completeness.

Professor Bobby Graham, who became a dear friend to me and my family through the years, taught me how to become a better soul winner, student of the Word and how to become a good pastor to the people. Dr. John O'Cain allowed me, as a young green preacher boy, to preach in his pulpit many times to give me experience. It was during this semester that I really began to see how much prayer would be a part of my journey through the rest of my life as I followed my Savior in the ministry. You see, in the ministry, pastors must depend on the Lord for everything and to continue on until their prayer is answered.

CHAPTER THREE

Well, after much prayer during that first semester, a one bedroom apartment became available to us. We were twelfth on the list, but the other eleven couldn't move, so it was God's will for my family to move up with me. This also worked out for the new owners of my home, so now we were ready to move on with our new walk of faith.

With my family now together, the finances were running low. My wife was able to transfer to Ashville, N.C., with her company and a new life began for her too. After a few months and a close call with her driving over a mountain side due to the weather, we both decided that she was to stay home. I began working full time with the G.E. plant in Hendersonville, N.C., while I also attended school. By the way, remember my trip to Fruitland and the encounter with the State trooper? Well, I still had not quit smoking cigarettes, five months had passed and every night as I came home from work, I would smoke only one, just one. Marie did not know that I still smoked. One night late, on the way home, God began to speak to my heart. You see, for the first six months of school, I was never asked to pray or even read a Scripture.

So that night as I was talking to God about this and He spoke to my heart with words so clear, "Until you give me all of your life, I will not use you." I stopped the car on the side of the mountain road, got out of the car, threw away the cigarettes and I cried, *"Oh, God I don't want to give them up; but, if that is what you want, I am nothing - but you gave all of glory up for me, then I can give my life totally to you."* From that moment on, over forty-eight years, God miraculously cleaned me up and I never had a desire to start smoking again. He filled my desire to smoke with a greater desire to please Him and study His Word. That night I went home, woke up my wife and announced to her my victory. We both rejoiced even though she thought I had quit before then.

Well my days started at 8 a.m. in school until noon, then lunchtime and finally off to work at 2:30 p.m. I came home around midnight. Yes, long days, trying days, yet great days and many hours of prayer went up just for physical strength and finances.

Many times, for the next three years, so many prayers were answered. I need to share some of these with you so you can see how God can and will stretch your faith.

During the next three years, I had the privilege to preach just about every weekend for pastors who were sick or on vacation, or for churches without a pastor. Needless to say, this put a strain on our finances, and yet, God never failed to provide what we "needed." I remember one special time that Dr. Booth came to the apartment around five o'clock in the afternoon, on a Saturday. He wanted me to go the Bat Cave Baptist Church to fill in the next day for both services. Well, I was excited to preach, to say the least, at this church at his recommendation; but, we didn't have the extra money for the gas to take us through the next week. Marie and I prayed and asked God to just "stretch" the gas a little farther. Sunday came, we went, God blessed; but, as we got ready to leave for the evening service, the car wouldn't crank. The battery was bad and darkness was coming. We prayed, pushed the car to get it started and then prayed up the mountain that the battery would hold out for the lights to show the way. What would we do after the service? Well, we would pray about that later. The evening service went well; the people were so cordial and kind to this green preacher kid. It was now time to leave for home and fear crossed my mind about our car. Would it crank and would the battery hold for the lights until we got home?

As we got ready to leave the church, one of the men came up to me and said, "I know you need some financial help so here is a little love offering for you." Wow! It was enough to buy gas for the next two weeks! Then he said, "We knew you needed a new battery, so while you were preaching we bought you a new one." Once again, God knew and worked through men all because of prayer, faith and His promise that "He would not let His children beg bread."

There was another time when our finances ran real close, in fact, we had nothing with which to buy groceries. All we had was a little flour to make a few biscuits, of which my wife did not make good ones until then, she became a professional at it. All we had for a couple of days was biscuits for the children. After school one day, Marie met me to walk me back to the apartment. I'm sure she came with questions as to how we were going to feed the children now for the next few days since we were out of flour and pay for their lunch at school. As we were walking down the path to our apartment, she said to me, "Honey, what is that against the door?" With excitement we both ran as fast as we could and found over ten bags of groceries and yes, an envelope with money to buy gas, and provide lunch money for our children for the next month! Only God could have done this! By the way, after being in the one bedroom apartment for less than six months, a two bedroom opened for the same cost.

The next month, I was hospitalized with pneumonia and had not one dime of hospital insurance. The bill was twelve hundred dollars. When they discharged me they asked if I could pay at least one hundred dollars each month until it was paid off. Of course I could only answer, "I will try." I was discharged, went home and began to pray for the strength to go back to work so I could make up the three weeks that I missed and somehow keep my commitment and testimony. I went back to work the next week on a limited basis, knowing that I needed all I could get. Marie and I never told anyone about the agreement with the hospital.

Amazingly for the next twelve months, every month on the day the bill was due, there was an envelope with a hundred dollar bill in it - in our mail box - with no indication of who it was from. Wow, God does answer prayer!

The Thanksgiving of 1968 we were not going to get to be with our families in South Carolina because of the lack of funds to drive home. On campus someone had given coupons and food for a Thanksgiving meal to two families and we were one of them. The other couple was also from South Carolina, so we decided to spend time with them and make it a "South Carolina Thanksgiving." The last day of school this same student came down the hall calling out my name loudly. Everyone on the hall was grabbing at me with excitement. He had received enough money for him to go home for Thanksgiving. Of course I was excited for him; but, it turned out he had enough for us to go home too. He shared it with my family and so to South Carolina we went. Once again, God stepped in. Before we left, we found out that a student couple did not have anything for Thanksgiving, so we gave them our food and yes, even half the money so they could have a wonderful Thanksgiving too. By the way, before we left to go back to school after church that Sunday, my home church took up a love offering, the first and only one they ever gave me. Yep, it was enough for us to get back to school and then some. Time went on and God gave me an opening with a company in downtown Hendersonville, N.C., with more salary, less working hours and a greater opportunity to witness each day to customers.

Those three years went by so quickly. God had used me so many times to preach His Word and even let me do interim work at a church under the leadership of Dr. R. P. Hamby, my New Testament professor and friend. He was also my senior not only in age, but in the knowledge of the God's Word. For six months, he helped me get more experience on the ministry of being a pastor. At the same time I was asked to become a "fellow in the Greek class" with Dr. Alex Booth. Graduation time was coming soon; but, I really wasn't looking forward to graduating. I didn't want to leave the area and my close friendship with the "spiritual giants" in my life.

Time was now coming fast to graduation and so many prayers had been answered. Marie was now working for the

Missions Director of our local Baptist Association and enjoying every day of it. The children were growing physically as well as spiritually. In November of 1969 I was called to be the pastor of a local church and we were so excited. I was ordained by the Fruitland Baptist Church of Hendersonville, N.C. By the way, that is where Charles Stanley was pastor prior to my moving to Fruitland. I had just started as pastor and we were looking for the Christmas of 1969 to be the first without facing a financial crisis since our arrival in 1967.

It was Friday and the last day of school before the Christmas holidays. I was sitting in my first class around eight o'clock in the morning when I heard an announcement over the class speaker asking me to come to the dean's office immediately. As I walked down the hall, Dr. Booth came running towards me with this announcement, "Marie has been in a terrible accident." This was strange news to me, for I saw her leave the apartment, which I could see from the classroom window, just five minutes earlier. He said it happened just around the corner. I immediately ran out of the building following other men that had seen the accident. When I arrived, I could not believe my eyes. Our car was in a ditch, totally demolished. It was a cold wintry morning. There was a heavy snow that night and freezing rain. Marie's car slid on the ice and another car came around the mountain curve and hit her side ways. As I got to the car, one of my friends said that I did not need to try to get to Marie, because she was being helped by another classmate. But being her husband, I wanted to get to my wife.

Yes, I was scared out of my mind. When I crawled into the car, the whole right side of the car was totally gone from the impact. As I got behind Marie, I could tell she was unconscious, yet moaning, and I knew she was in serious condition. My friend said, "You better hold on to this, they will need it." It was her left ear. I grabbed a hand full of snow and covered her ear in it until I could give it to the EMS team that was on the way. It seemed like an eternity for the EMS to arrive. As they removed Marie from the car, I saw more.

Her face was totally "chewed" up since she had hit the windshield at least four times. The glove compartment and a three foot piece of chrome were embedded in her side and her legs were under the driver's seat. I heard many that saw her say that she will never survive. We were rushed to the hospital where they immediately began working on my wife to save her life. Within minutes, many of my fellow students were at the hospital to stand in a prayer vigil with me. They began a prayer chain all over North Carolina. It seemed that they were working on my wife forever. Finally, the head surgeon came out and said they were going to do X-Rays to see what the damage was to her back. He felt that she would never walk again or maybe not even survive.

More prayer went up. After the X-Rays were done and the men were still praying, the doctor came out and walked towards me. Then he turned around and went back into the room and then came out a second time. Once again, he went back to the room. Well, you can imagine what I was thinking. When he came out the third time, I was there ready to stop him. He looked at me and with tears in his eyes he said, "It's a miracle, it's a miracle. She does not have a broken back or broken limbs only her chest will need some time to heal." GLORY TO GOD, I shouted, and the whole emergency area was in tears and praise. They finally took her to a room. Her face was so mangled that our children couldn't look at her. Of course, we began praying for her complete healing. Now for those that do not know my wife and those that do, when you look at her after all these years, you would never know her face was in such dismemberment. By the way, she never had any facial reconstruction or surgery. PRAISE THE LORD! There is a lighter part to this story. Our children were taken to friend's home. After Marie was resting and it was about eight o'clock in the evening, my dear friend, and professor, Bobby Graham, took me to supper to a cafeteria down from the hospital. While we were there, many friends and strangers came up to give me their prayers and then one couple came up and said, "We are sad to hear about Marie and that you are taking it so well." "Well," I thought, and then they said, "Her passing." I jumped up, left Bobby, ran to the hospital, up the stairs to her room expecting to see the worse, and all I heard was this horrible sound... SNORING! Yes, snoring, she was sound asleep. Bobby was right behind me and what laughter came from the both of us. She was fine.

So, as the famous Walter Winchell would have said, *"and now the rest of the story."* Since this was the only car we had, we had no transportation. We prayed for the Lord to provide us with some type of vehicle. The day after the accident I received a visit from a local car dealer. He brought me a brand new car to drive, with the only "catch," that I could have it for one week. The next week I could get another car and so on until I settled with the insurance company and could buy another one. It did not take long for the settlement of the car and until then I had the use of a brand new car, gas included!

Well, after prayer of what kind of car to purchase, the dealer brought me a brand new station wagon and all but gave it to me for his cost. Again, prayer was answered.

Marie recovered quickly and was brought home to begin months of healing. It was now time to give my attention to pastor a full-time church, in Hendersonville.

❧ 4 ❧

_____

Our First Church and Coming "Home"

_____

CHAPTER FOUR

꙼

I had only been pastor of a local church there in the Hendersonville area for a short time when the accident happened to my wife and the church rallied around us as well as the school. It didn't take long for Satan to work his damaging deeds as we began our work. As Marie continued to get better, I was able to go visiting more to reach the lost and minister to our church members; but, my heart wanted to reach the lost.

One area I felt called to get involved with was reaching the teens in the high school near our church. We were able to begin a Bible study and I began to make close contact with many business people in the area. God began saving many souls. The church began to grow little by little over the next few months and once again in the church waters began to stir but not in a positive way.

I encouraged our leadership to begin going out once a week visiting in the area around our church and inviting them to church. As a new pastor, I was surprised to see the hesitancy and response.

I knew then, that it was not going to be easy to be an aggressive, evangelistic pastor for you see their main focus was ministering to the members. This was an old established church in name only but not in growth and outreach. I realized that I would have to be the one to do the leading in this area, so every Saturday morning I would go visiting all day, two nights every week to try to be an example. Not much response was given, and I remember what Brother Bobby Graham said to me about being a pastor, "the time will come when you will have to be a loner in building a church and never give up even though you want to." I have never forgotten his remarks and lived it many times in forty-three years.

It was one morning while visiting high up in the mountains I came upon a home that was certainly not one I would have wanted to live in. As I drove up to the house, there were about six dogs lying in the yard.

I had a fear of being attacked, yet the Holy Spirit moved me to get out. With fear and trembling, I got out and not one of those dogs even gave out a sound. Well, victory! As I approached the house, three little children came out to meet me and I cannot begin to describe the sight and smell of that home and the children. As I stepped on the porch, I was greeted by a young mother carrying another small one. After a lengthy conversation, she agreed to come to church on Sunday, if we would pick them up. Sunday came and we went up the mountain and picked up the young lady and her four children. As soon as we entered the building, I sensed they were not welcomed by the nursery workers due to their appearance. After some convincing the teachers, the children stayed in the appropriate classes and the mother attended our church services. When I gave the invitation, this young mother came forward and got saved. She asked if she could get baptized. What a joyful day! One of the ladies of the church lived close by and said she would go get her a change of clothes. This young lady got baptized in the coldest water I think I have ever been in. When she came up out of the water, there was such a glow about her that only the Lord could give. Yes, we were rejoicing; but, Satan was not ready to give up.

After the service, before we took them home, one of the deacons asked to see me when I got back with the other men. The bottom line was, "don't bring them back to church, they don't fit in." Well, Satan had left his mark. We had the meeting and I gave them my resignation. I simply could not begin my ministry under such indifference of a group of leaders. Only six months of being a pastor of my first church, not a good start, huh?

It was now only a few weeks until graduation, and I had nowhere to go. We had to vacate the living quarters on campus right after graduation, according to the policy.

During the week after graduation we were not able to find a place to rent so our children went home to South Carolina with my parents. Marie and I stayed in the dorms until we could get some direction for our future. Around the middle of the week, I received a telephone call from a member of the pulpit committee in Darlington, S.C., where we lived before I entered Bible College.

Marie had continued to heal physically and emotionally. We both knew that God had opened this place for us. We quickly and with great excitement headed to South Carolina with all of our belongings.

I was under a little pressure because I had played ball against some of the members of this church. One of them was their coach and there were some, well, "heated" activity during these games. Only a ball player would know this feeling. The weekend at the church and the committee went so smoothly. It seemed that we and the church had the same goals and purposes for the growth of the church. In only a couple of weeks I was called to become their pastor and I knew that God was going to give us a great ministry, a local man coming "home."

The church received us with open arms and immediately we began a visitation program, promoted a strong Sunday school and youth programs. I learned something quickly that I need to pass along to young pastors, don't let your zeal outrun your leadership and followers. Even though many say they are ready to go, they don't mean grow!

This should have been an easy move but when my former company heard that I was coming back to the area, they sent word that they wanted to see me when I arrived. Well, after a short time with the personal director and my former supervisor, I was offered a position as their "trouble shooter." It was good to know that after three years they still wanted to use me. But remember, I was now a pastor. They offered me a part-time position and with a great salary package that certainly would help with the small income from the church. The wonderful thing was, I could even come to work at will. After much agonizing prayer, I had to turn them down, for I knew Satan would win that war. I also remembered that I committed my life to my Savior "full time." Regrets, none! Now it was time to - not look back – but, go forward with the heavenly calling.

This was in 1970 during the times of the "hippie era" and the Vietnam War. I began to visit all of the church membership, family by family. I was called on to help with my first church funeral. I remember calling one of my professors and asking him to help me with the message. I wanted to use the one that Jesus had preached.

He chuckled and said, "Brother Gene, Jesus didn't preach any funeral services. He just raised them up from the dead." Well, I knew I couldn't do that, so he gave me some Scripture references and helped me out. I was still being taught, even after finishing school, and I am still being taught by the Holy Spirit how to study. I also had my first wedding service and began reaching out to the "hippie" groups in the town. It was exciting, people were getting saved, young couples began attending, teens began coming and the Lord added to the church. In September of that year, we went to the first Bible Conference at Thomas Road Baptist Church in

Lynchburg, Virginia, where Jerry Falwell was pastor. What a week! I was exposed to a ministry that I never knew existed. That week just added more fuel to my spiritual fire. I was exposed to men like B. R. Lakin and Doug Oldham. I learned about the "bus ministry" and "junior church." I heard a choir with such power and wonderful talent; but, the greatest of all was the challenge to go back home and win my city for Christ kneeling on the ball field in Lynchburg with hundreds of pastors. Well, I went back with a new zeal and again, Satan began to work.

We encouraged the church to buy an old school bus to begin a bus ministry. Of course that caused some "hair rising" from those that thought we were going "modern." We brought in a "Karate team" from Liberty during the Southern 500 race week and even had a float in the parade. Everyone in the area would clap and cheer for our float as it went by. I thought it was because of our kids until I found out that behind us was the grand marshal, James Arness, the famed TV star from "Gunsmoke." Well, even with this "let down," we had a wonderful week of revival until Satan began to rise up his head, again.

Trouble began and I was accused of being too "liberal" and "modern." The leadership of the church began to challenge me about the messages I preached, the outreach program, spending too much money and not keeping money for "rainy days." The list went on. It was during that time that God blessed us with the birth of our third child, a little girl, Tracy. For a while problems calmed down, but only for a while, when again, men of the church kept on challenging my leadership as dictatorial.

After much prayer, we decided to resign and seek another place of service. A dear friend and physician, who delivered our third child, came to our aid and asked me to start a weekday ministry (HIS - His In Service) for the older adults in the town. Until God gave us a church, we did and it launched a great ministry in town.

During the meantime, we stated attending Florence Baptist Temple and after a while, I was asked to come on staff to head up their bus ministry. For over a year, I learned much from the pastor and in 1973, God led us to Marion, South Carolina, to start a new Baptist church. This was certainly going to be a definite step of faith for two reasons:

One, we were not taught how to start a new church at school and secondly, I had no income to take care of my family for the upcoming months. Now a new chapter in the Schuyler ministry was about to start and a "school of prayer" was about to begin, because I had never dreamed of starting a new church.

કે

5

Stepping Out by Faith to Start a New Church

᙭

O ur move to Marion was definitely a move of total faith in our Lord. Afraid? Yes, but we knew this was what God wanted for us so we sold our home in Darlington. With enough money for three months rent on a house, car payments, food and a place to start the church, we arrived in the little country town of Marion, South Carolina.

Talk about a new experience! They never taught me in Bible school how to start a new church. So here we go Lord through open doors!

The first step was to locate a house to live in and we did just that. After settling down in this new area and not knowing any one, we began to just walk up and down the streets of Marion and Mullins (a neighboring town) telling people of our desire. We never asked anyone that attended a church to come to ours. We had yet to find a place to meet; but, if they did not attend a church,

I got their names and addresses and promised to contact them when we did. Well, the first week we reached only one family, a young mother with two children. I was still seeking a place to meet. Would you believe in that week I found a most logical place to meet? A funeral home! That's right, a funeral home. The owners had recently built a new facility, so we rented their old building for our first Sunday. With a couple of coffins in the back room, we launched the BIBLE BAPTIST TEMPLE OF MARION, SOUTH CAROLINA.

So, on our first Sunday, we met with that young lady, her two children, her mother and my family of five. The offering was enormous, $14.00. The rent was $10.00. Hey, we had four dollars left! So here we were ready to tackle the world.

The next week when I went to ask for permission to use the building for the next couple of months, I was told they could not rent to us anymore. After much pleading, I found out that pressure was put on them to not rent to another church, "that there were enough churches in the town." Was the door closed for me? NO! I was not going to give up. So on that Wednesday, the folks that came on Sunday met with us at our house and we began praying for a place to meet. For the remainder of the week we drove around looking, but to no avail. We met the next Sunday in our home. The next week we continued the search for a building. As we looked, we found an old cricket farm.

Yep, you read right, a cricket farm that we heard was going to be available in a month. Now to those that have never seen or heard of raising crickets, it was quite an experience for me also, since I was a city boy.

The building had only a few old fashioned ceramic light fixtures that just held small wattage bulbs. There were many caged containers with thousands upon thousands of crickets growing. The building had no windows and only one door. I went to the owner and was told that there were nine more people ahead of us in line for the building. The owner was very cordial and sympathetic to us. He was a Christian and had never heard of someone starting a church so it drew his interest; but, he had to keep his business focus. After our talk with him, Marie and I knelt at the entrance of that building and claimed that place for our church. We did this every day for the next two weeks. In the mean time, we found a very small church that only met once a month so we got permission to rent from them when they were not meeting. Some of their members came to hear me preach during the next four weeks. What a glorious blessing!

One night near the beginning of the second month of waiting, I received a phone call from the owner of the cricket farm. He said, "All of those wanting the building backed out. You can rent the building." GLORY TO GOD, HE ANSWERED OUR PRAYERS! By this time, the young lady that started with us got her husband to come to church. He got saved and her father was saved as well. We found a family living in Marion that was driving to the Florence Baptist Temple. With their pastor's encouragement, they started visiting with us. We moved into the cricket farm with now 12 people attending. Does this number sound familiar?

Wow, a place to call our own, but there were a few problems. The light fixtures needed to be replaced with more and better lighting. The building had a concrete floor and there were no bathrooms, no air conditioning, no chairs and no pulpit. In other words, it was nothing but an empty building. It would take faith in the One who sent us to do His work.

So, when we started that Sunday, we had six first-time visitors and there was nowhere for them to sit. Now the faithful new ones that had just started with us brought their own chairs. They gave up their chairs for our guests. We were off and running except for not having adequate lights, air conditioning or restrooms. It was now June and summer was coming.

After talking with our guests, I had leads on two families that might be good prospects. On my first visit, I met a man who

CHAPTER FIVE

was drinking a beer and wasn't interested. His wife was on the porch and she accepted Christ as her personal Savior. The next visit that afternoon, the gentlemen was very cordial and said he was looking for a new church. Wow, he had no idea how new we were. Well, I went home so excited, thinking about our first new converts and a potential new member. We were not a church yet officially, but we were on our way.

That next Sunday we had over 30 in attendance. The young lady that was saved the day before was there and her husband came too. Remember him? Well, God blessed even though they had to bring their own chairs. We still had to endure the babies; but, God kept them quiet. When the invitation was given, this young lady's husband came rushing forward weeping and saying, "Please tell me about Christ as my Savior." Great day! Revival broke out that morning and everyone came forward and prayed for God to do it again every Sunday. PRAYER WORKS!!!!

For the next few weeks we took special love offerings to buy more and newer lights for the ceiling, 40 of them, and an air conditioner for the summer. You would have thought we had had a hundred thousand dollar building. Within the next week we had our own church telephone. By this time the city was buzzing about this new church in the "cricket farm."

Well, time moved on and after six months in our cricket farm, we were able to purchase 75 chairs, new lights, carpet for the floor and a piano (on time payments-our first investment). We were given songbooks by a sister church. We were really moving on! A new problem arose; we needed more income. I did not have a job. I wasn't receiving a salary from the church, so I had to start seeking employment.

God used my experience in the secular world to open a position in the local area. I was able to work full-time and still have the evenings to visit and study. Before I was hired, I told the supervisor I was starting a new church and could only work first shift. Again, God answered prayer.

For the next six months God blessed our church and we began growing so fast we couldn't keep up with the growth. I couldn't keep up with the visiting either. I prayed and asked God to give me direction about going full-time and quitting my job. He did and the church took me on full-time. What excitement there is when God answers prayer.

We bought our first bus, then our second, and when we went to purchase our third one, the group that we purchased our first two from, when we bought the third one, gave us the fourth one—FREE! God was really showing us how He works when we stay faithful.

One of our promotions to get the attention of the city was to place in the local newspaper the following: "ARPO." That's all it said. The next week I put "ARPO IS", the following week, "APRO IS COMING", and then the next week, "ARPO IS COMING TO BIBLE BAPTIST TEMPLE ON_____," then I put the Sunday. Would you believe our little building was full and at the end of the service I announced what "ARPO" was: "Advertising Really Pays Off." I know, I know, a little "corny," but it worked, we had over 20 visitors that day!

Time went on and we were now averaging 100 in Sunday school and over 150 in preaching. We had new families with babies but no nursery or restrooms. Well, after much intense prayer, God sent us a mobile home to use as our nursery.

My sister-in-law let us use one that she had and you would have thought we had been given a $50,000 nursery. Our youth ministry began to grow and we need space, so Brother Larry Upchurch let us borrow a large tent from his church that would hold up to one hundred and we began to grow in number with young people. As time went on we grew in the children's ministry and again out of space in the cricket farm. You see, we hung "bed sheets" dividing up the building during Sunday school hour for adults and children and then pulled them back for the preaching services.

We then went to the owner of the building and asked permission to add on to the building two restrooms and a room for the children for Sunday school. He gave his permission; but, the only problem was, we didn't have a building fund or money to do the project.

Again, it was time to pray! I went to the local bank to secure a loan to help us add on to our old cricket farm building. After giving all the necessary information they required, the loan officer said, "You and all your church are not worth loaning you any amount." Well, I was so glad that I was saved for the old nature wanted to take over; but, God and the men that went with me, held me back. We left and the men asked, "What are we going to do?" I had announced that in the coming fall we would have a Christian school and we were adding on a new building for growth. My last remarks to the gentleman at the bank, were, "Just wait and see what God is going to do and you will want our business."

After much prayer, I went to the bank where we had our checking account and told my dream to the president. He was a Christian and agreed to loan us enough to add on to the cricket farm building. We now had our first loan. Amen!

God continued to bless us. Great interest in the church began as I preached on separation, salvation and second coming of the Lord, and the Lord added students to our Christian school. Again, God blessed, not only within our church family but in the community as well. God answered our every prayer and by our second anniversary we were starting a new Christian School, yes in the cricket building. We raised enough money to prepare our building to meet the requirements of the Christian Educations system that was called ACE education. I went to Texas for training and came back to open our K-5 thru 10th grade school with over 75 students. Our great God sent teachers who sacrificed to help us make this dream come true for our community.

We had made a mark in the area as a Bible-Believing Baptist Church. God blessed us with many special groups and guests during our first two years. Evangelist George Grant better known as "Gorgeous George" on TV wrestling, Mayor Cooper Tedder of Florence, S.C., and Lee Hayes, the radioman of the "USS Pueblo" which was captured by the North Koreans in 1976. Many well-known singing groups and Bible College presidents paid a visit to our church too. Our folks were blessed to have such great people of the Bible as Dr. Curtis Hudson of Atlanta, Georgia. He helped us with our first stewardship program and banquet. He would not accept any money for coming to be with us and this was during the recession. Brother Larry Upchurch, my pastor now, came many times; by faith to be able to buy gas to get back to Raleigh, came to help us with our second stewardship program, "Together We Build." It was during this campaign that we began to look forward to our first building program.

God began to bless in such a great way during the next year that we began to outgrow our location. I knew that we were not able to purchase the location we were at so we began to pray and seek land to relocate. About that time, something happened that we did not expect, we were going to have our fourth child! Can you imagine our surprise? My wife was now thirty-nine years old. We had two teens and one little girl three years old. The members of our church began to call us "Abraham and Sarah." My wife was doing so well that she continued working with me as my administrator of the school until little Rebecca was born in August, 1975.

During this time we kept looking for land but to no avail. To be honest with you, I began to wonder if we would ever be able to find land. One night when we met with the contractor that was building our new house, I casually asked him if he knew where I could find some land to build on. After we finished our meeting, he remembered the question I had asked him about the land. He took out an oblong lock box, opened the lid and out spring deeds to land he owned in the area. He said, "I think I have a little piece of dirt here that might interest you. Let's take your family home and then come with me." I took my wife and children home.

The contractor and I continued our travel. I followed his directions very carefully and finally, after about a fifteen minute ride, which seemed like an eternity, he told me to stop the car.

He asked me to look to my right and there was the most beautiful, flat, not one tree around "piece of dirt." My, did my heart speed up! Could this be the place? I knew we could not afford this land though. He invited me to get out and we walked the road frontage and he asked me "How much land do you think you would need?" I was so excited that at first I stuttered, and then it just came out: "at least five acres and maybe more later on." Then he said, "That's fine." I asked him, "Do you know who owns this land?" Then I heard the most wonderful statement, "I do." Then I asked the big question, "How much?" He responded with "How much do you have on you?" What a question! I asked him to repeat his question and again it was the same, "How much do you have on you?" I looked in my wallet and responded, "One dollar." He said, "Sold." I could not believe my ears, "Sir, did you say sold?" "Yes" was his answer. Then he said, "When you need more land just let me know." I first fell on my knees and thanked my Lord for such a miracle. Then I shook the gentleman's hand, hugged his neck and then jumped a ditch. I began running all over the land, crying, shouting and praising God.

Then I heard his voice saying, "Preacher come on back I want to call my lawyer to get the paper work going tonight. You can come back tomorrow and run all day long." Dear friend, God did perform a modern day miracle for a new church. During those days there were no cell phones, so I had to wait to take him home and then drive home to share with my wife and family what God had done. We went back out to the land in the dark and just sat there and cried and praised the Lord.

This was on a Friday and I couldn't wait to tell our church. What a day it was that Sunday when I announced that we now owned five acres of land and they only cost one dollar. Talk about excitement and shouting we almost became "bapticostal."

I had already had the plans for the new building rough drawn and we now needed the money to begin building this miracle building. As we began our road to this adventure, we decided to float bonds to finance the building. I hired a bonding company to help us start the process. The gentleman came to start the program on a Sunday after weeks of promotion, and during the service he made this statement, "if you don't buy a bond it is doubtful you can go to "Heaven." Without a moments hesitation, I jumped up and told him he could not talk to my people like that, and that was not scriptural and I sent him out of the building. Later on in the afternoon the company called and tried to apologize but I would not let them continue on. With this happing, I took on the responsibility to sell the bonds with the help of training our people. It did not take long to put together a prospectus in the amount of $125,000, to build our dream for our Lord. We followed all of the requirements of the Security Exchange Commission and God blessed and the SEC approved our plan and selling of the bonds, so off we went. The total cost of the building that would house the church and school facilities would be nearly $125,000.00. We secured a building contractor, a Christian group, and we did well the first few months.

Let me share with you how God stepped in and taught me more about faith and prayer. One day when I stopped at a local gas station that I only visited now and then, the owner asked me if I had any more bonds to sell. "Of course," I said, "How many do you want?" He asked me to come inside the station. I was shocked when he gave me ten one thousand dollar bills. I couldn't believe my eyes, and responded, "Are you sure you want to do

CHAPTER FIVE

this?" He smiled and said, "Preacher, you have done a great job in our little town and I want to be a part of it." Stunned, I said, "Keep the money until I get back." Then I called our church treasurer and had him meet me at the station. Both of us took the money to our bank.

We saw miracle after miracle. As we neared the completion of the building and grounds, we came up short $25,000. The contactor said he needed the balance before he could finish the job. I tried to sell the rest of the bonds but it seemed that the end would not be near. Then the Lord spoke to my heart to go see our banker. Off I went to tell our banker of our need. He called a meeting with the board within the hour. We met and one of the members of the board asked, "What is his security?" You must remember we did not own anything but five old busses, 150 chairs, and some school equipment. The response from the president was, "The preacher's word and God's backing." The board agreed to give us the money and we were able to complete the building.

At this time, we were nearing July 4, 1976, our nation's 200th birthday. We were planning a special day at church. On that day we were shooting for our goal of 300! Our highest day ever was 176. More than this, we were going to meet in our new building and it was not yet completed. The walls were up, the roof was on, but it was not really ready for occupancy. We promoted we were going to meet at our new location for that day only for a celebration. We rented a large highway billboard and we were the first church to use a billboard in that area. We invited everyone to celebrate with us on July 4th. When Sunday came 200 metal chairs were in place and the nursery, the piano, and the platform were all ready too. We recorded over 500 in attendance and many souls were saved.

As soon as the services and the meals were over, the rains came. You have never seen so many people running for cover.

The members loaded up the furniture to move back to our old location for the evening services.

Well, the word got out around town about that Sunday and more people came to see this miracle. The following months after we moved in during September, 1976, the banker that said we were not worth anything monetarily showed up the very week that we occupied our building! After a tour of the building he asked if we would consider moving our account to his bank. Graciously, and this was hard for me, I told him no thanks and I shared with him this story.

"Texas football coach Darrell Royall was asked as they prepared to play for the national championship which quarterback would start. At the beginning of the year the first and second string quarterbacks got hurt and Darrell had to use his freshman to run the quarterback position. When the championship game was to be played, both the first and second string quarterbacks were healthy again. As Coach Royall said, "I am going to stay with the one who brought us to the dance." In other words, no thank you, we will stay with the bank that stood by us when no one else cared about us.

It wasn't long after that day that Satan once again, went on the attack. He planted some folks in our church that began causing problems. Some of our folks started doubting our church's work. There were attacks on the school as well.

During this time, I became sick and was hospitalized for a week. No known reason was diagnosed. For a time, things begin to get better and revival began to start again within the hearts of our people. Easter of 1977 came and God blessed greatly, like when we first started out. The attitude of the church was more spiritual and soul conscious again.

That following Friday, after a hard week at church and working with the school, my family and I went to eat supper at a pizza restaurant. We had a wonderful time and Rebecca, the baby, was just twenty months old. That night she was just unbelievably funny. It was the first time she had ever eaten pizza. As we started to leave the restaurant, Marie and Rebecca began walking away from the rest of us. When I called out to them they seemed to be in another world. Finally, Marie responded and they came to the car. Marie said something just kept telling her to keep on walking; but said to Rebecca, "We must turn around. Daddy and the children will leave us." Normally, we would have gone window shopping; but, everyone was tired and we had a revival coming up next week and arrangements needed to be finalized. We laughed all the way home talking about how Rebecca acted. She was our little angel. She brought a lot of joy to all our hearts that night.

Within the next three hours, Rebecca went to Heaven. I will never forget that day and neither will my family and I trust no daddy will ever have to witness the death of any of his children as I did. Only twenty months old and now she was gone! My world was totally destroyed and so was my family's. Talk about how strong your faith is; mine was tried but never doubted and neither was my family's. It is amazing how people respond to tragedy. The next morning, after Rebecca's death, friends came to console us. A preacher friend came to see us and I began to cry as he asked what happened. To my shock, he responded by saying, "Now brother, you cannot let your people and friends see you emotional, for you are a pastor you must be an example."

I held my temper, and breath, and responded, "Brother, today I am not a pastor, but a grieving father." Immediately he apologized.

Make sure you mean what you say or sing to the Lord for you just may be called on to live it. On the Easter Sunday before Rebecca was killed, I sang a song entitled, "Whatever It Takes to Draw Closer to You Lord." One of the stanzas was "take the dearest thing to me, change my life, my plans, for whatever it takes....." After the funeral on Sunday, we left for Raleigh, N.C., to spend some time with one of Marie's sisters. We stayed until that Friday and then headed home. All the way home I couldn't get peace. I questioned my calling and whether we should stay with the church. I even entertained quitting the ministry.

When we arrived in Florence, S.C., just about forty minutes from Marion, I stopped the car and told Marie, "I can't go back and get in the pulpit again; I need God to give me peace and strength." We got a room at a local hotel. We could have stayed with my parents for they only lived five minutes from the hotel, but I needed to be alone with God. After we had eaten supper, we went to our room at around six in the evening; Marie and Tracy, our youngest child, went to sleep. I went out on the little deck off of the room and all night I prayed and cried out to God and asked, "Why?" And for hours upon hours I wrestled with God and read scripture.

Nothing gave me what I needed. It was around six in the morning that I finally said, "God unless you give me something soon, I am going home to resign not only from the church, but I am going to quit the ministry. Then God led me to Second Peter chapter five and verse ten. That was what I needed to help me go on. After forty-three years I am still serving my Lord and Savior.

With that settled, I awoke Marie and Tracy and we headed "home," to a house without that little miracle baby. The following months for all of us were very difficult to adjust without the "baby." Marie and I talk often of what a day it will be when we see Jesus and then when we will walk all over Heaven with Rebecca.

It was only four weeks after Rebecca's funeral that our Christian school participated in the annual competition. I was one of the speakers. As I sat on the platform waiting to speak in a few minutes, another of the speakers leaned over to me and asked this question, "Which of your four children would you had rather God taken?" What a horrible question! I breathed deeply and responded, "I am so glad that I will never have to make that decision." He then replied, "Forgive me, I wasn't thinking." It was very hard not to retaliate later on. I just asked God to give me strength not to doubt His will with Rebecca and our family. I don't know how I spoke; but, He saw me through it by His power.

The weeks began to go by with healing and getting ourselves deeply involved with God's work. We had only been in our new building for a year and it was recommended that we name the children's wing in honor of her memory. After talking with the deacons and some of the church members that had started with us they thought it would be a great move. The wing was dedicated and it wasn't long before some of the "new" church members became very critical of the dedication. They didn't want to make "Rebecca into an idol." As you can imagine this caused Marie, our other children and me much sorrow and hurt. Many people began to lose confidence in me and my leadership. The church began to go down in attendance and offerings. I was totally destroyed. I had given five years of my life to them and sacrificed in many ways to keep the church going. Had God taken His hand off me?

A number of the ones that I led to Christ and ministered to them began to ignore me at church and even in public. Until I get to Heaven, I will never know why all this happened after so many miracles from God.

છે

❧ 6 ❧
———————

A New Start in Kinston, NC

———————

CHAPTER SIX

❧

Not long after Rebecca's death, many rumors began as to why she died. To my sadness many of our members began to believe these lies. Pressure began building up. Satan was really gaining ground. Trying to restore the spiritual atmosphere was much more difficult than when we first started. Many of the members began to withhold their giving and follow the disgruntled ones that came into the church. The summer came and we were preparing for a new school year at the church; but, the enrollment was not coming in. Satan continued his charge. August came around and Marie and I were at the church working, me on the ministry and Marie on school enrollment, hiring teachers, and calling parents to see if they were going to enroll their children again. A terrifying call came in from our oldest daughter with these words, "Daddy, the house is on fire!" All I could say was, "Call 911 and we are on our way." It was about a thirty minute drive to our home and as we approached the house, all I could see was heavy black smoke. Our hearts sank. As we got near the house the fire department stopped us. They recognized me and allowed us to get a little closer. We ran to the house and with great relief saw all three of our children were alive and well. My son told us that our four-year-old Tracy, now our youngest again, was upstairs asleep but he got her out before the fire reached her bedroom. Once again, we asked, "Lord why?" Once again, the rumors began! Needless to say, in the days to come, battles were raging with Satan and even with some of our church members. I didn't blame them then and still don't. They were so young in the Lord and Satan knows just how to operate on young believers.

For the first time in our five years at Bible Baptist Temple, the church God had led us to start and where many, many miracles took place, I began to doubt my calling. I spent the next weeks agonizing and praying as to what to do and how to handle this adversity. God settled the doubt about my calling, but I still wasn't sure if He was through with me in Marion. I sought help from some pastor friends and did not want to hear their words of advice, "God is through with you in Marion, leave."

Well, that sounded like good advice; but, couldn't God have dealt with me in another way rather than take our little daughter in such a tragic way? Why did He allow our house to burn and almost let our next to youngest child die all in only five months? "Dear God, **HELP!**"

To my surprise, within a few weeks we got a call from a church in North Carolina about the possibility of becoming their pastor. Now the battle really began to start. Should I leave the church I knew God had called me to start or was this a move of Satan? Well, I went for the interview and preached a revival for them later on and was called to become their pastor. Somehow, I still wasn't one hundred percent sure if this was what God wanted me to do. Marie was still hesitant about going and I tried to convince her that God was in it due to the ninety-eight percent vote of the church to come. They had a large Christian school, and it was a church of historical victories. It was a place that we could heal from the hurt in losing Rebecca. So, we accepted the church's offer and off we went to a new adventure.

After being there only three weeks, I was approached by the chairman of deacons with this announcement, "Next week we have to go meet with the IRS." You see, for years they did not pay the social security of the employees of the school. The amount was in the double digit figures and the officers said they were not going to pay it!

Well, after legal consultation, we had to sell some of the church's real estate. In the meanwhile, we did not know just when the IRS would call for the amount due. I made arrangements with a local bank and they agreed to loan us the money until we sold the amount of real estate necessary. This was another miracle because I had never met the officer of the bank and we didn't have our accounts in their bank. The time came and we paid off the debt; but, I wasn't sure that the church owed the entire amount. After a good attorney took our case and spent a few months of investigating, we were able to get back one-third of what we paid. That was another miracle. With this major hurdle over, we began doing what God's church was supposed to do, reach people.

God blessed us within a few months at the new ministry, but I could not get Marion off my heart. I had heard that the pastor they called to our church in Marion left not long after he accepted the church. The next pastor that came sold all of the buses and closed down the school. I "drowned" myself in our new church ministry and tried to forget the church that I had birthed.

God began to bless. Souls were being saved and the church was growing at a rapid rate. The school began to grow too and then Satan began to rise up his ugly head again. My two oldest children were bombarded with the pull of the world and we faced situations that we never thought we would face. To top that off, we had a bomb scare at the church one Sunday morning. The police searched the building; but, they did not find a bomb. To make matters worse, numerous threats were made on my life and my family for about two months. Things settled down after they caught the one that called in the bomb threat. We did not nor did any of the church members know the person responsible.

The devil continued his attack when some of the deacons tried to find fault with us. They thought that I did not live up to the former pastor with my preaching and were critical of how I handled the administration of the school. They began looking for ethical and moral issues in our personal lives; so, they went to Marion to find something that they could hold over my wife and me.

Why did we ever want to move to North Carolina and be their pastor? I found this out and called a meeting with those that went. They became hostile and words began flying and the old nature started again; but, **GOD STEPPED IN**, and gained control. The meeting ended with no peace. Again, "was this a wrong move on my part? Did I leave Marion without God's approval?" In less than eighteen months I resigned the church under pressure. "Well, here we go Lord, what next?"

I tried hard to keep the "peace" within the church and to keep the school in a positive way with growth. I seemed to step on toes in many areas of the church and school policies. I even had one of the members approach me one night after service in front of the church and made the statement that "God had called him to keep me straight." Thankfully most of the church ignored him and we kept on going until Satan continued the harsh attack against my family with many accusations. Finally I just couldn't take the pressure and resigned my position as pastor. That evening a number of members came and asked me to start a new church in Kinston, for those that wanted a real Bible church. I agreed and we located a small place on the edge of town, and began visiting, yet we never addressed any fault in the former church or any of its members. We floundered and grew some; but, my heart was filled with questions about why we had to go through so many valleys.

CHAPTER SIX

The newness grew cold and many went back to the other church and we had to move to a local mall due to a smaller cost of meeting. We met and we did reach a few people, but it just seemed that I never could get peace about this new ministry; it wasn't like it was when we started in Marion. I began to ask "God, will I ever be able to continue in the ministry?"

Back in 1972 I met Larry Upchurch at a conference in Lynchburg, Virginia, and we became close friends. He was such a help to me when we were in Marion and guided me as we made decisions in our new ministry there. So through the good and sad years, we stayed close. I called and even met him many times for advice and prayer over the situations we were going through. One day he called and asked me to meet him half way to Raleigh.

At the meeting, he asked if I would consider coming to Mid-Way to help him as a staff member. After a few weeks of prayer, I agreed and a new page in our ministry began.

ॐ

❧ *7* ❧

A Ministry of Evangelism and Growing

CHAPTER SEVEN

&

J anuary 1980, we arrived in Raleigh at Mid-Way Baptist Church to begin a new chapter in our ministry. I served on the staff as the Minister of Evangelism and for the next three years, God really blessed me with the wonderful family at Mid-Way. It was during that time that I received a telephone call from the former treasurer of my church in Marion. The church was going bankrupt and he wanted me to come down and try to help them.

Oh, how my heart broke! In the meeting with the bank and bond holders, it seemed to be inevitable that the church was going to go under and dissolve. I gave my bonds that we had purchased to the church and so did many others; but, it wasn't enough to satisfy the bank. I was encouraged to come back, take over the church and rebuild it. The problem was, somehow one night; someone got rid of all of the pews, classroom and sound equipment. In other words, it was "gutted." I declined to take back the ministry because I could not bring it back since it had such a bad testimony in the area. Once again, I was advised not to take the church back but just let it dissolve. To this day, I regret not going back to the church that God led me to birth.

I continued to serve Mid-Way until July of 1983 and left to start a new work in the Myrtle Beach area. For two years it was a difficult time building a new church in that area. We were in a financial crisis in America and it was very hard to meet the financial needs for a new church and for me and my family. God did bless us though and over 100 were saved through that ministry. There were times that we did not have enough money to buy groceries. Marie and I had to go to work in a Christian school to survive.

To us, a visit to McDonalds was the highlight of the month. Christmas was coming and we knew we could not afford to get our little girl anything for Christmas. Our two older children had now grown up and left home. All Tracy wanted was a Cabbage Patch doll. We could not afford it; but, we could afford the doll kit. Marie patiently, in her "spare" time, secretly made the doll for her. That was all she got for Christmas of 1984.

In September of 1985, we were asked to come back to Mid-Way and we served there for another three years.

In 1988 under the advice of Pastor Larry Upchurch, I took a church that was in bankruptcy. The attendance was less than 50 but they had an auditorium that seated 1,500...that's right 1,500. Their Christian school was also floundering.

For over a year we lived off my personal credit cards and gave most of my salary to pay the teachers.

Then in 1989, our little girl gave us the news that she was "engaged." We were happy for her; but sad, our last child was now leaving us. She left an empty spot in our hearts; but there's joy too, for since then, she and our other two children have given us eight grandchildren and now five great grandchildren. Yes, God took Rebecca; but, He has given us back abundantly, like He did for Job of old.

Things were going well, but financially it was still hard. In 1990 God performed a MIRACLE for our church. Our auditorium could seat 1500; but, we were running around 175. Remember now, when I took the church we had less than fifteen on the first Sunday I was pastor. After praying with the deacons, we made the decision to sell the property and relocate to a facility that would meet our needs. Within 30 days after our decision, a local church that was really growing in the city was interested in our property. After many meetings and much prayer, we agreed to "do a swap." Their building would meet our needs and our building would meet theirs.

The lawyers on both sides say they have never seen or heard of a transaction like this one. We were able to pay off over $200,000 in bonds that were many years past due -- that was another miracle. I personally called every bond holder to announce to them they were getting an early Christmas present. Their checks had been overdue for years.

We also got over $50,000 in cash and a clear title to their old facility that was appraised at nearly one million dollars.

During this time we were informed by our youngest daughter that they were expecting their first child. This was exciting for us, our youngest now going to be a mother. Things went well at first. Then she began to have some problems in carrying her child. After a meeting with a local physician in her city, she was told it would be a "down-syndrome" baby and they recommended that she have an abortion. My daughter took a stand by saying she would not kill her baby and that God would give her and her husband the strength to raise this child if it was to be. Well, we found another clinic in Atlanta, Georgia, and an appointment was made for more tests and after a period of time the good news came, the baby was going to be just fine. It would be normal; another Miracle for this family.

Well, wouldn't you know, Satan went on the attack again. Before the deal that I mentioned afore was even "dry" on paper, rumors that I had the title to the property put in my name started. I could not convince these parties of the truth; so, I had our attorney try to convince them that it was a legal transaction and the title was in the church's name.

Well, by that time our church attendance was growing and now the fight was on. This matter never seemed to die. After counseling with friends in the ministry, I decided to leave. During this time, Brother Larry Upchurch encouraged me to come back to Mid-Way and in the latter part of the month of August 1990, I went back on the staff of Mid-Way Baptist Church.

Over the next three years God once again blessed my wife and me with spiritual healing. After three years at Mid-Way, somehow, a church received my resume. I never sent it out; but, they called and asked to talk with me. After four months of meeting and preaching a revival for them, I received a ninety percent vote to come. I accepted. It was hard this time to leave Mid-Way, for they had really been such a support for us, but I knew that God had this for me.

❧

❧ 8 ❧

A New Beginning

&

W e arrived at this church in July of 1993, with excitement and the assurance that God had placed me there until He came for the church in the rapture. The church was debt free and attendance was around 150.

Within only six months we began to run over 250. Souls were being saved every service and we began baptizing every other Sunday. Pastors were coming on Wednesday nights to see why we were having such a good attendance on Wednesday nights as well.

It was during my ministry here that our youngest daughter was expecting her second child. Something unexpectedly happened: trouble! We were called late one night to come to where they lived in Athens, Georgia. We were told of the complications and I immediately tried to contact the chairman of the deacons but could not. I called my secretary and gave her the information and we left for Georgia. Well, not one officer called me during this time and our new little grandson lived only a few hours and then went to be with God. This was another death of a child in our lives and I saw the faith of our daughter, like her mother, become real. Our other two children came to her side and supported and encouraged her and us.

Sad to say, I still did not receive any word from any officer of my church expressing any sympathy. Only my secretary contacted us. When I got back I was told that I had no right to leave without approval from the "men." This led to other accusations; then, it happened again. Satan was fed up with what was happening and on the attack he went. After being pastor for only eleven months, I was asked by the deacons to leave by way of a letter in the mail. They did not have the courage to face me and ask me personally or even call a meeting to discuss it. I took it to the church that Sunday and gave them a week to talk about it among themselves.

The majority followed the leadership of the deacons and I resigned. I was asked by those that wanted me to stay to start a new church; but, I knew that was not what God would have wanted me to do.

I also knew I could not go through another church split. Where do I go from here? No home to move to, my income would be cut in 30 days -- once again, God why?

We packed up and moved to my hometown to live in my father-in-law's old house and begin all over again. It was in pretty bad shape. My wife, who stood by me all the way with all we had gone through, was my cheerleader, supporter and encourager. She immediately found a job; but, it took me over two months to find something. Everywhere I went I was told I was too qualified to work for them. Yes, even Wal-Mart turned me away.

I sent out so many resumes that I couldn't keep up with the churches that I had sent them to. No response from any of them. "God, are you through with me now?" Even though Satan seemed to have the victory, for now, I wouldn't give up. I kept on praying and believing and remembering what Dr. Vance Havner told us one day while we were at Fruitland, "Keep your eyes on and faith in God." Then he gave me something that I have never forgotten. He gave me the acrostic of FAITH—*For All I Trust Him.*

Time went on for about three months and I finally got a job as a shoe salesman at Rack Room Shoes. I thought to myself, "I will become the best shoe salesman God ever had." Well, except for D. L. Moody. For over a year, I sold shoes and enjoyed every hour because I got to witness to so many people with problems. It is amazing when you just show kindness and interest in people they will share their hearts. At work I led four of the sales personal to Christ. During our time in our hometown, we started going to a church that I attended when I was just a little junior boy in Sunday school. The pastor, whom I did not know, took me under his "wing" and became a very close friend and prayer warrior for me during this time. He even let me preach for him when he was out of town.

During this year Marie and I became teachers for the teens and saw many of them come to know Christ. While there, it seemed that I would never get back into full-time Christian ministry again.

God continued to bless us there and I was offered the position to manage the store. I turned them down for I knew in my heart that God was not through with me.

One night after a long day at the shoe store, I received a call from Brother Larry Upchurch asking if I was willing to come back to the Raleigh area and help a pastor with his church. After a number of meetings with the pastor and search committee, they called me as their associate pastor.

God gave us a good ministry there for four years and when the pastor resigned, due to his declining health, he stated in his resignation letter that he wanted me to assume the position as pastor. I had a great rapport with the people, yet Satan popped up his head again. The deacons took over as the pastor search committee. They ignored the pastor's request and informed me that I would not be considered for their pastor.

Again, God had another plan for me and my Marie. The very week that I was told that I would not be considered for the church pastor, I received a call from a Christian school in Maryland. They had received my resume and wanted me to be the administrator of their Christian school. Once again, I do not know how they received my resume, but they did. We went for an interview and that very same weekend they extended me the call. Off we went on another adventure and divine appointment with God.

The school was well established and they wanted me to take them to a higher level. They wanted to be an accredited school. God opened many doors to help us get the school where they wanted in only one year. Many of the students came to know the Lord as their Savior, as well as their parents. I don't know how we made it financially, because we were still paying on our home back in Raleigh, leasing an apartment in Maryland and taking care of my mother back in South Carolina with her needs.

As the end of the year came to a close we had accomplished so much. Eighty percent of the teachers were now certified and the school was to be finalized the next year. They had never had a mascot for their school and now they were the "Eagles" soaring for Christ.

My wife and I had decided that we might be where God was going to use us until He came for the church. My mother, who was back in South Carolina, was in bad health towards the end of the school year. She began having symptoms of dementia and I had no choice but to move back and try to take care of her. For one year we tried; but, my mother became worse and eventually became a victim of Alzheimer's disease. Sadly, we had to place her in a constant care home until her home going in 2006.

She followed my Godly father who went to be with the Lord in 1999 with bone cancer. What now? No ministry, both parents gone to glory, one child in heaven and now this. Both Marie and I were under stress both physically and mentally; but not spiritually, for we knew God was not going to let us down. We knew that He had a place for us.

છે

❧ 9 ❧

One More Time

&

W e left for South Carolina to help mother for the one year in 2000 and began seeking God's will for our lives. Once again the question, what is God going to do with the Schuyler's. Mother seemed to be doing better, so we moved back to Raleigh to our home and began seeking God's future for us.

Marie was able to go back to work with the company that she had worked for many years without any penalty for the year she was gone. She was able to keep all the benefits and time with that company. What a blessing!

I continued doing pulpit supply and substituting in a Christian school when called upon. I kept seeking God's face for my future. I will never forget the morning when my wife called me and asked me to turn on the television in time to see the second airplane crash into the second Twin Tower in New York City. 9-11 will live forever in the minds, hearts and history of America.

It was just two weeks after that day that another church called to ask for me to come and talk with them about becoming their pastor. After three meetings with the pulpit committee the church voted to call me as their pastor. I was told that I received ninety percent of the vote. This would come back to haunt me in a couple of years.

After the first year of the ministry there we began to see some growth. This was an old established church that did not have a history of growth. This growth caused some of the members to be uncomfortable. On the first anniversary of 9-11 we had a special service at the church in honor of that day. God richly blessed. We had over 300 people present - - including local dignitaries, military leaders and officers, the local sheriff and others. The chaplain for the Eighty-Second Air Borne Division presented me a special medallion celebrating the 9-11 date. We received a great newspaper write up. Wouldn't you know it, you guessed it, Satan started up again! Why? God was moving in this little town. It was the same old story once again: "too evangelistic; too showy."

To them, I was giving too much time to others and not enough time to the church members. I tried to cut back on soul winning; but, my heart was - - to reach the lost.

May 4th came and I received a call from my wife's friend at work that Marie was very sick. I asked her to take my wife to the hospital because it would take me an hour to get to the hospital. After the initial visit with our family doctor, we were advised to take her to the emergency room. Marie was examined by a cardiologist and the diagnosis was she needed open heart surgery. What a shock! There was no time to waste and so my wife had three by-passes and came out a champion. She recovered in the required time and was released to go back to work on July 20th.

Let me say here, not one officer of the church or one person visited her while she was in the hospital or visited in our home while she recovered or even asked to help in any way.

On July 30th, just two months after my wife's surgery, I was diagnosed with a heart attack. Yes, only two months after my wife's surgery, I had to have five by-passes. Once again, history almost repeated itself. I did have two men call me and still not one person came to visit me in the hospital or at my home. In fact, when told that I would be out that first Sunday, they called a supply pastor without me knowing it. God blessed and I was back in the pulpit only four weeks after the surgery, but I knew then that I was on the way out.

Almost a year went by with more opposition from leadership in the church, but I still did not bend to their "philosophy" of how a church should be run. In May of 2004 I was informed that they knew I had started receiving Social Security benefits. They never actually asked me if I was. They cut my salary based on their estimation of what I should receive from Social Security. By the way, the church had grown numerically; but, all the new people who were attending were rudely run off. I began feeling the pressure and my health began to be affected. My cardiologist recommended I should resign or I would suffer a more severe heart attack and maybe not survive. I tried to continue as pastor and prayed the attitude would change - - but to no avail.

In April of 2004, at a Wednesday night monthly financial meeting, I was made aware that many church members were coming that night that had not been in months or even years. They planned to vote against any proposed budget and to ask for my resignation. Before the meeting started I opened in prayer and then read my resignation and my date of departure as pastor. I was not going to put my wife through any more stress or heartache. Now here came another year, what would we face?

ॐ

❧ 10 ❧

Back to Our Knees and Looking Up "One More Time"

&

For a couple of weeks I floundered around seeking to get some direction on what God would have me to do. I began to ask questions of my wife about starting a Christian school in the Fuquay-Varina area. Would it work? Was it God's will? I had no finances at all to start this school and no income either. Even though Marie was still employed that would only meet our obligations…barely.

So, by faith, I took enough money to place an advertisement in the local newspaper. I bought a ream of paper and printed five hundred flyers asking about those interested in being a part of a Christian school in the area. I contacted a local hotel, rented a room and got in touch with the area director of ACSA to meet with us. He explained why accreditation was important and answered other questions about Christian education.

I already knew the answers; but, I felt that having someone of his caliber would be an advantage for us. We had a good number to meet and express interest so I announced the time for the next meeting to find out who really was serious about Christian education.

During the meantime, I found a local Bible Church that was willing to help us by letting us use their facilities to start the school. They only asked us to pay the extra expenses they would incur each month. What a blessing! I was also given an office to work from at no expense to me. All I had to do was to add a separate phone line for us to use and not ask the church to answer any questions.

At our next meeting, we met at the church with approximately 40 interested parents and shared the blessing from this local church and went over our policies, educational expectations from the parents and students and our responsibilities to the students and parents. We all knelt and prayed that God would give us the number of students we needed to get us started.

Understand now, we were going to start with K-5 thru the twelfth grade! What a step of faith; yet, I wanted to make sure God was in this and it was not just me wanting to do this. I told those attending the meeting that I would need at least 50 students to begin this work.

Our next step was to raise money so we could offer salaries to potential teachers and for operating expenses for one complete year. I did not intend to take any salary for the first year. The total amount came up to quite a budget; but, I wanted to raise this amount before the doors open to start the school.

I sought the help of a local business man that I had served with on a board of trustees for a local Christian TV station some 20 years before. I went to him and shared my dream. He gave me quite a large sum of money and which seemed to be a great start for us. Surely God was in this. Later that week, a former member of church that I had pastured heard of my plans and gave me another good amount. All I needed now was students to start enrolling, paying all the necessary fees and their first months' tuitions.

We had another meeting with those that had pre-registered their children; but, it was not enough to get us going. We again prayed for the number we needed and set a time that would be the date to make the final decision. This was in March of that year and we had to have the number by July to make it a go. During this time, I went to the city planning commission to let them know of our plans and asked what I had to do to make this plan acceptable. After making the application, they sent a team to inspect the church building. They determined that it would take almost a complete remodeling of this building due to its age (the church was able to operate because of a grandfather clause – we were a new operation). It was way out of reach for me to raise that much money before the school could start in September.

I had to make a hard decision; but, I was not going to start this school in a negative way and have a testimony that would not be pleasing to my God.

I called those brave parents that took a step of faith with me and told them the sad news, "The school could not start due to the enormous amount of money needed to make it safe for operation. We did not have enough students to carry the basic operating costs either."

I refunded every dollar we received for pre-registration. We had no debts outstanding. I was not about to hire teachers and staff and not be able to pay their salaries on a month to month basis. The dream of a Christian school had to have been mine and not the Lord's.

After refunding all tuitions and fees and paying of all expenses, I had a little over two thousand dollars left. Another battle started between me and Satan. He whispered, "That money should be yours. You earned it for the work you did. It is rightfully yours." Well, I was not about to let that happen; but, I did not know what to do with this money. I wasn't a member of a local church; in fact, we had not joined a church since I resigned. During the months we tried to start this school, I visited many Baptist churches. I met with the pastors in the area to help get their support. Not one showed any interest in a school except the non-denominational church that was willing to let us use their facilities.

September came and we started visiting Baptist churches in the area. Not one pastor contacted me, even though I filled out the visitor cards as only a visitor and not a pastor. Now how would you feel? Time passed and it was now approaching the first of December. I still had the surplus of the money after paying off all expenses; so, I contacted the businessman that gave me the first large offering. I told him why the school could not be started and asked if he wanted the remainder of what was left back. He quickly said, "No, give it to missions." That was good advice, but to which church? The ones I had attended seemed to have no interest in me as an individual. They certainly were not interested in visiting me to see if I was a prospect for their church. After praying about what to do with this money, the Lord told me to go to Mid-Way again. It was time for the "Chest of Joash" and He told me to put all of what I had left towards their goal and keep nothing for myself.

On the first Sunday of December, 2004, Marie and I went back to Mid-Way just to feel the presence of the Holy Spirit and be a part of wonderful people that I had known for many years. As we dropped our offering and the money left over from the school into the chest, Pastor Upchurch asked that we get together for lunch the next week.

After our lunch together, Brother Larry listened to what had transpired in the last few years of my ministry. When Marie and I both had heart surgery he was always there to support us, even though we were in another city. He asked if I would like to come back on the staff at Mid-Way in a part time position. I would work just two days a week in the area of outreach. (I now work four days a week; but, I am always available twenty-four seven.) I never dreamed that I would come back as a Mid-Way staff member since I had been gone for eleven years. I accepted the offer and in January 2005, I once again became a part of the Mid-Way staff and church family.

At this writing, I have now been back at Mid-Way for almost six years, which makes a total of eighteen years we have spent with this church family that loves the Lord and Marie and me. I now have the privilege of serving as Mid-Way's Membership Pastor. What has God got in store for me in the future? Whatever HE wants! What about you? Walking by Faith is His Way! "TOTAL SURRENDER."

SERMONS

Gene Schuyler has preached a series of messages on CD at Mid-Way Baptist Church that covers a broad range of topics. The following is a list that is available:

- Today's Events-Prophecy and the End Time
- Questions you have always wanted to ask but. . .
- Rejoicing in Revelation
- The Christians Highest Calling – Worship
- Great Doctrinal Stones of the Faith
- Teachings from the Master
- Born to Win and Not to Lose

These are available by calling:
Gene Schuyler at 1-919-552-6023

Or write to:
Gene Schuyler
P.O. Box 1521
Fuquay-Varina, NC 27526

❧ *Sermons* ❧

I have placed a few sermons that the Lord has given me to use that I hope and pray will be a help in your walk by prayer and faith.

Sermon # 1

The Importance of Prayer and How to Pray

John 15:4-7; I John 2:28

In verses 4-7 we find the word "abide" seven times and we are told not to just remember His Word, but that it is to remain in us as a living principle to regulate our actions and life.

What then is the meaning of our Lord's promise? One must remember that God does not give us a blank check. For if this were true, many times this would be injurious to ourselves as well and be dishonoring to our God.

Then the question comes, **"Why pray?"**

John gives us the answer with two conditions that qualify the promise that we find in verse 7.

1. Abiding in Christ signifies the maintaining of heart communion with Christ.

2. Not only must our words and our heart be occupied with Christ, but our lives must be regulated by His Word, fed by faith and hidden in our hearts.

   Psalm 119:11. One must realize that prayer is not to be occasional or spasmodic, but a habitual and continual communication with our God through His Word until it becomes the substance of our innermost being.

Now this brings us to **How to Pray.**

To understand this truth we will find in Mark 11:24 three factors that are vital to our prayer life.

1. The Desire Factor

   With the desire factor there are four qualifications to make a prayer of any value.

   a. There should be definite objects to plead for:

      ❖ Opportunities to witness daily

      ❖ A closer walk with your Savior

      ❖ Health

   b. There should be an earnest desire for its attainment. In other words, do we really want to grow in Christ and attain our maximum victory?

   c. There should be a firm faith in God.

   d. There should be real expectation from God.

2. The Direction Factor

   We find in Isaiah 55:6 that we are told, *"Seek ye the Lord while He may be found, call upon Him while He is near."*

3. The Determination Factor

   This leads to a wonderful passage of Scripture that will give total victory through determination.

   In Jeremiah 33:3 we find God's wonderful invitation for us to pray.

   1. A Command that comes with the promise. What an invitation!

2. A Confidence that comes with this promise. "I will answer you."

3. A Conquest that comes with this promise. "and shew you great and mighty things which thou knowest not." God can do anything and He promises:

   ❖ That there are no problems that He cannot solve

   ❖ That there are no promises too hard for Him to keep

   ❖ That there are no persons too hard to save

Always remember that God has invited us to pray. Not to pray to the one who saved us and has given to us eternal life is an insult. Friend, it is time to pray!

❧

Sermon # 2

Power Walking

I Thessalonians 4:1-8

Paul wanted the people in Thessalonica to excel in their walk with Christ in the walk of faith. What is this walk of faith?

1. You have been reached by God. Are you reaching out to others to share the gospel message? Chapter 1:4-10

2. You have been fed with God's Word. Are you feeding others? Chapter 2:8 gives us a command to disciple others. Are you?

3. You have received instructions from God's Word. Are you excelling as you should? Chapter 4:9-12

4. You have been encouraged. Are you encouraging others? Chapter 5:11

ॐ

Sermon # 3

Our Christ of Every Crisis

Acts 12

Have you had any troubles today? Well, we all do and sometimes we don't know where to turn unless we turn to the Lord. The greatest crisis I have ever faced was the death of our 20 month old daughter in 1977. Let me give you four thoughts on how to face a crisis in your life.

1. Always respect the mystery of the providence of God.

2. Always rest in how God masters peace.

3. Always request the ministry of God's people. Acts 12:5

4. Always rejoice in the power of God's majesty.

ॐ

Sermon # 4

Are You Unconditionally Surrendered to the Word of God?

Romans 1:1-16

1. Are you faithful to the obligations of the gospel? Vs. 14

2. Are you flexible for all of the opportunities of the gospel given to you? Vs.15

3. Are you fearless in face of all opposition when given the gospel? Vs. 16

ॐ

Sermon # 5

A Call to Readiness

I Thessalonians 4:16-17

When one deals with or talks about the return of Jesus, it never fails to create mixed emotions. Look up:

Matthew 24:42-44 and Acts 1:11

The fact remains that JESUS IS COMING!

While we wait for Jesus, there are four observations that will give us guidance:

1. We must be well informed.

   We know what our Savior has revealed to us about our future. He gives us confidence about our present state.

2. We arc not to grieve or be nervous with those that have no hope.

3. We all must face death without fear for Jesus Christ is our example.

4. We must be aware of the order of the events of His return and then we must:

   ➤ Occupy-Luke 19:11-27

   ➤ Purify-Titus 2:11-14

   ➤ Watch-Mark 13:32-37

   ➤ Worship-I Corinthians 11:23-26

ॐ

Sermon # 6

This sermon is what the Christian life is all about.

Preached at Mid-Way Baptist Church, Raleigh, N.C., on December 12, 2010.

Text: Galatians 2:20

Introduction:

As I stood on the deck of the USS Missouri a few weeks ago in Pearl Harbor and read the "unconditional Surrender of the Japanese nation," of which many of our younger generation has no full understanding of its importance and meaning. It brought to my mind the passage of Scripture that I just read, that many of the saved have not understood its truth, or have rejected the meaning intentionally.

So for tonight and as we get ready for a new year in just a few weeks, I wish to address an important subject for every born again believer: The Difference between Committed and Surrendered...When you are committed, you are in control; but when you are Surrendered, someone else is in control!

Why is this verse so important to me? Because it gets to the heart of the most essential matters of the Christian life. As F.B. Meyer puts it, this is Paul's "confession of the power of the cross in his own life." It stood between him and the past. His self-life was nailed there, and this new life was no longer derived from vain efforts to keep the Law, but from the in dwelling and [overflowing] of the life of Jesus -- the perennial spring of John 4:14.

It is important that as we look at Galatians 2:20, we need to examine **the context, the content, and the challenge** of this matchless verse.

SERMONS

I. The Context of This Verse

Look back with me to verse 11......... The whole background of the confrontation between Paul and Peter is beyond the purpose of this message. In fact, too many "unknowns" have boggled greater minds than mine. What is clear is that Paul "stood up" to Peter for a good reason. Peter was to be blamed. He was acting not only against his conscience but, more importantly, against the revelation he had received from God (see **Acts 10 and 15)**.

What stirred Paul's holy indignation was the **deceitfulness and compromise of Peter**.

In Antioch Peter had shared meals (including, perhaps, the Lord's Supper) with non-Jewish Christians. Everyone knew this and rejoiced. Peter was the first apostle to evangelize Gentiles (Acts 10,11,15) and was, therefore, to be trusted. **But when "certain men came from James** [the pastor of the Jerusalem church]...he withdrew [from this fellowship with Gentiles]...fearing those who were of the circumcision [Jews]"(2:12). This disorderly behavior **seriously influenced** "the rest of the Jews" [in the church] who "played the hypocrite with him"-- **including Barnabas**, who "was carried away with their hypocrisy" (Gal.2:13).

Such deceitfulness and compromise were more than playacting; they were, in fact, an adverse reflection on the gospel of the grace of God and unity of the church of God.

By his bad example, Peter was implying that Gentile believers who were saved by grace alone, through faith alone, needed to "live...as the Jews" (2:14), and that law-keeping and circumcision rituals were necessary for acceptance by God. **This was, in essence, heresy!**

Whatever else we can say about Peter, he was dodging the message of the cross! For as we shall see in a moment, **to be justified by the grace of God is to die** -- as far as the law is concerned, so as to life -- as far as God is concerned.

And this is not the first time Peter was rebuked for dodging the crucified life. It happened after his great confession at Caesarea Philippi. What could be clearer than his words "You are the Messiah, the Son of the living God"? So sound and fundamental was this declaration that Jesus said to him, "Blessed are you, Simon son of Jonah! For flesh and blood has not revealed this to you, but my Father in heaven."

Yet shortly afterward, when "Jesus began to show His disciples that He must go to Jerusalem, and undergo great suffering at the hands of the elders and chief priests and scribes, and be killed, and on the third day be raised," we read that "Peter took Him aside and began to rebuke Him, saying, 'God forbid it, Lord! This must never happen to you!'" But the Lord "turned and said to Peter,

'Get behind me, Satan! You are a stumbling block to me; for you are setting your mind not on divine things but on human things.'"

Peter's refusal to accept the way of the cross eventually led to the shameful denial of his Lord -- even after boasting that he would lay down his life for Jesus' sake (John 13:37; see Matt. 26:30-35; Mark 14:30-31; Luke 22:31-34). But that was before Pentecost and, therefore, somewhat understandable.

<u>But for you and me there is no excuse since we have the Holy Spirit</u>. And yet we are living in an hour when the message of the "crucified life" **is the last thing many professing Christians want to hear. They adore the cradle of Christ and await the coming of Christ, but they abhor the cross of Christ.** For many religious people, the cross is either a stumbling block or a laughing stock (1 Cor.1:23).

2. That brings us to the Content of this Verse

This verse, dear Christian, is the great doctrine of justification by grace through faith. This is the true Gospel. It is also the principle article of all Christian doctrine. **<u>Listen:</u>**

❖ **Jesus Christ came into the world to live and to die. In His life His obedience to the law was perfect. In His death He suffered for our disobedience.**

❖ **On earth he lived the only life of sinless obedience to the law which has ever been lived.**

❖ **On the cross He dies for our law-breaking, since the penalty for disobedience to the law was death. All that is required of us to be justified, therefore, is to acknowledge our sin and helplessness, to repent of our years of self-assertion and self-righteousness, and to put our whole trust and confidence in Jesus Christ to save us.**

"Faith in Jesus Christ" then is not intellectual conviction only, but personal surrender.

The expression in the middle of verse 16 is (literally) "we have believed into Christ Jesus."

It is an act of surrender, not just assenting to the fact that Jesus lived and died, but running to Him for refuge and calling on Him for mercy.

So justification is not only a legal fact in which we are declared righteous by a holy God; **it is also a transforming experience through a living identification with Christ (v.17).** By union with Christ we are radically transformed; we can no longer go back to our old life, for in Christ we are "a new creation" (2 Cor. 5:1).

This brings us to:

3. The Challenge of This Verse

Read verse 20......... In this matchless statement Paul the apostle encapsulates the gospel of the grace of God. It is the gospel of the extinguished life -- "I have been crucified with Christ" (Gal. 2:20). The message of this book is so necessary for true over comers in the Christian life.

We have died to the law. **By dying with Christ**, who died under the law's penalty, we find that **all the law's demands were satisfied in Him**.

❖ **Being crucified**, moreover, means that we have died to self. The dominating control of the fallen nature has been broken. **If we do not understand this, then we are missing something very important. The extinguished life means death to self and sin.**

So in Galatians 2:20 we have the gospel of the extinguished life.

❖ But it is also **the gospel of the relinquished life** -- "It is no longer I who live, but Christ lives in me" (Gal. 2:20). No longer is our life self-centered but Christ-centered. By the ministry of the Holy Spirit, the Lord Jesus lives out His life in us day by day as we maintain total dependence on Him. The apostle says the same thing in his letter to the **Romans 6:13.......).** We do not relinquish ourselves to an enemy, **but we present ourselves as a bride to the bridegroom who has wooed and won us in love.**

As a pastor, I have had the privilege of marrying couples times without number. As the two stands before me, I say to the bride, *"Will you have this man to be your lawful wedded husband?"* She answers in two words, *"I will,"* and they are joined for life. **That is the kind of presentation we are thinking of when we speak of the relinquished life**. We are saying in effect, "Lord, I am married to You, being alive from the dead, to bring forth fruit unto God. Lord, from now on my language and life are two words: 'I will.'" Every day we must repeat that once-for-all interaction: "I am wholly Yours, Lord. Use me for Your glory."

Thirdly, it is the gospel of the distinguished life -- "The life which I now live in the flesh I live by faith in the Son of God, who loved me and gave Himself for me" (Gal. 2:20). That phrase, **"faith in the Son of God," is loaded with rich meaning.** Because of our union with Christ crucified and risen, we are "partakers of the divine nature" (2 Pet. 1:4); **we actually share with the Son of God the distinguished life.**

Two aspects of this distinctive life are spelled out for us. As the Son of God, our Lord in His perfect humanity chose to live a dependent life. He lived by faith (see John 5:19, 30;6:57;8:28; and 14:10). **We also must live by faith (Rom. 1:17; Heb. 11:6).**

The other distinctive is that the Son of God lived a devoted life. **He "gave Himself for [us]" (Gal. 2:20). That takes in the entire sweep of His life, service, and even death, in response to the will of His Father.**

In similar fashion, we are called to the high and holy distinction of yielding ourselves to God as living sacrifices so that we might "prove what is that good and acceptable and perfect will of God" (Romans. 12:1-2).

Dependence on God and devotion to God are the marks of divine distinction. Such distinctiveness can be detected anywhere and under any circumstances by a watching world. Out of such a life the streams of living water flow in blessing to others.

As God's people, we must be willing to pray and mean:

Crucified with Christ, my Savior,

I am dead to sin and shame;

Now HIS LIFE rules my behavior --

To the glory of His Name! Amen

ARE YOU COMMITTED OR ARE YOU SURRENDERED?

⌘

www.ingramcontent.com/pod-product-compliance
Lightning Source LLC
LaVergne TN
LVHW091314080426
835510LV00007B/486